It's a Baby...

Copyright © 2024 Vanessa Jarrett.

All rights reserved. No part of this book may be reproduced, stored, or transmitted by any means—whether auditory, graphic, mechanical, or electronic—without written permission of both publisher and author, except in the case of brief excerpts used in critical articles and reviews. Unauthorized reproduction of any part of this work is illegal and is punishable by law.

ISBN: 979-8-89419-536-0 (sc)
ISBN: 979-8-89419-537-7 (hc)
ISBN: 979-8-89419-538-4 (e)

Because of the dynamic nature of the Internet, any web addresses or links contained in this book may have changed since publication and may no longer be valid. The views expressed in this work are solely those of the author and do not necessarily reflect the views of the publisher, and the publisher hereby disclaims any responsibility for them.

One Galleria Blvd., Suite 1900, Metairie, LA 70001
(504) 702-6708

It's a Baby...

VANESSA JARRETT

Scene 1:

It's a baby...

Scene 2:

Cookout Scene

"Auntie Kisha, we're here for the barbeque!"

Scene 3:

"Mom you're getting fat, I'm going to call Jenetta Keg!"

Scene 4:

(ERIC JR): "Is this good or is it bad mom? It's hard enough sharing you with dad, now I have to share you with another little lad. And mom, there's no room on your lap any more. Does that mean I'm not your baby anymore?"

(MOM): "No son, you will always be my baby."

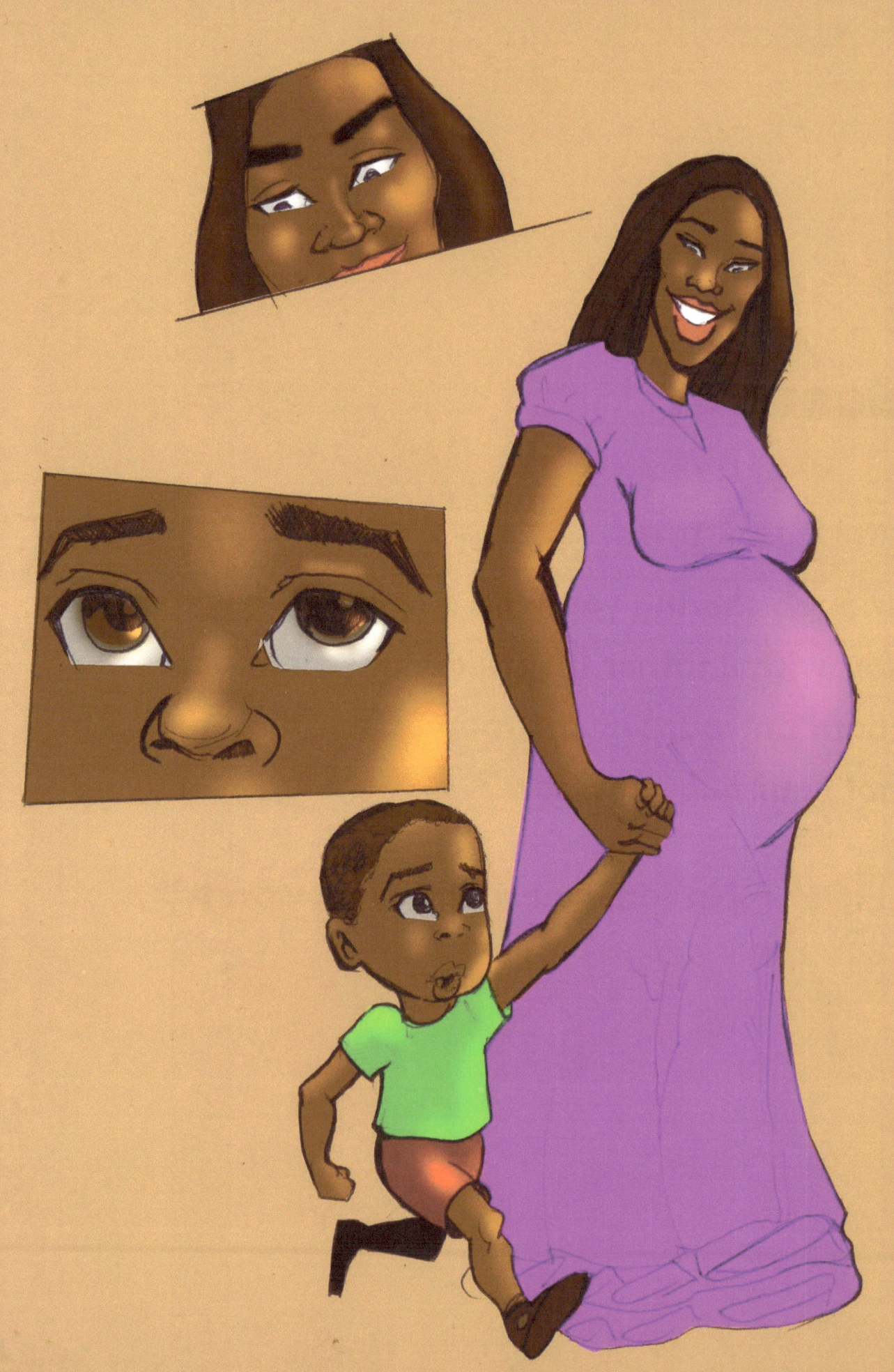

Scene 5:

(ERIC JR): "Mom what's happening to you and to me?"

(MOM): "It's called a baby."

(ERIC JR): "What will it do?"

(MOM): "Crawl, walk, and talk, just like you, Quincy, Derrick, and Judah. They will be your brother or sister. Whether it's a boy or girl, we don't know yet.

Scene 6:

(ERIC JR): "Mom, I love you this much! Do you think the baby can hear me?"

Scene 7:

(ERIC JR): "Did you eat the baby?"

(MOM): "No son."

(ERIC JR): "Then how did it get in your belly?"

(MOM): "This baby came from the love me and your father have for each other, so God planted a seed in here. Called a baby."

(ERIC JR): "That's how it got in your belly!?"

(NOAH - QUINCY - JUDAH): "I don't know how it got there, but I got to find out!"

(JUDAH - QUINCY - ERIC JR): "I hope it's a boy!"

(AKHIYAH - SHAUNESSY - AMAYA): "I hope it's a girl! Her name will be Vanessa."

Scene 8:

(ERIC JR): "I will give her hugs and kisses."

(OLIVIA): "Me and Mariah will do the dishes!"

(MALISSA): "I will baby sit!"

Scene 9:

(OLIVIA AND MARIAH): "We will play games with baby Vanessa and teach her girly things, like baby dolls, hair bows, and barrettes all over my platts. We hope it's a girl!"

Scene 10:

(MASON): "I will teach her how to ride a bike!"

Scene 11:

(NOAH): "Vanessa and I will play kickball!"

Scene 12:

(OLIVIA AND MARIAH): "We will be cheerleaders and have lots of fun! we can teach her every cheer we know as she starts to grow and gets older!"

Scene 13:

Kisha - Eric Senior - Mariah

(MARIAH): "I was wondering **WHEN!??** When will it come out!? Will the horn sound!? Will she shout **OUCH!?**

(MOM): "Honey, it's time!"

(DAD): "Okay, I will get ready."

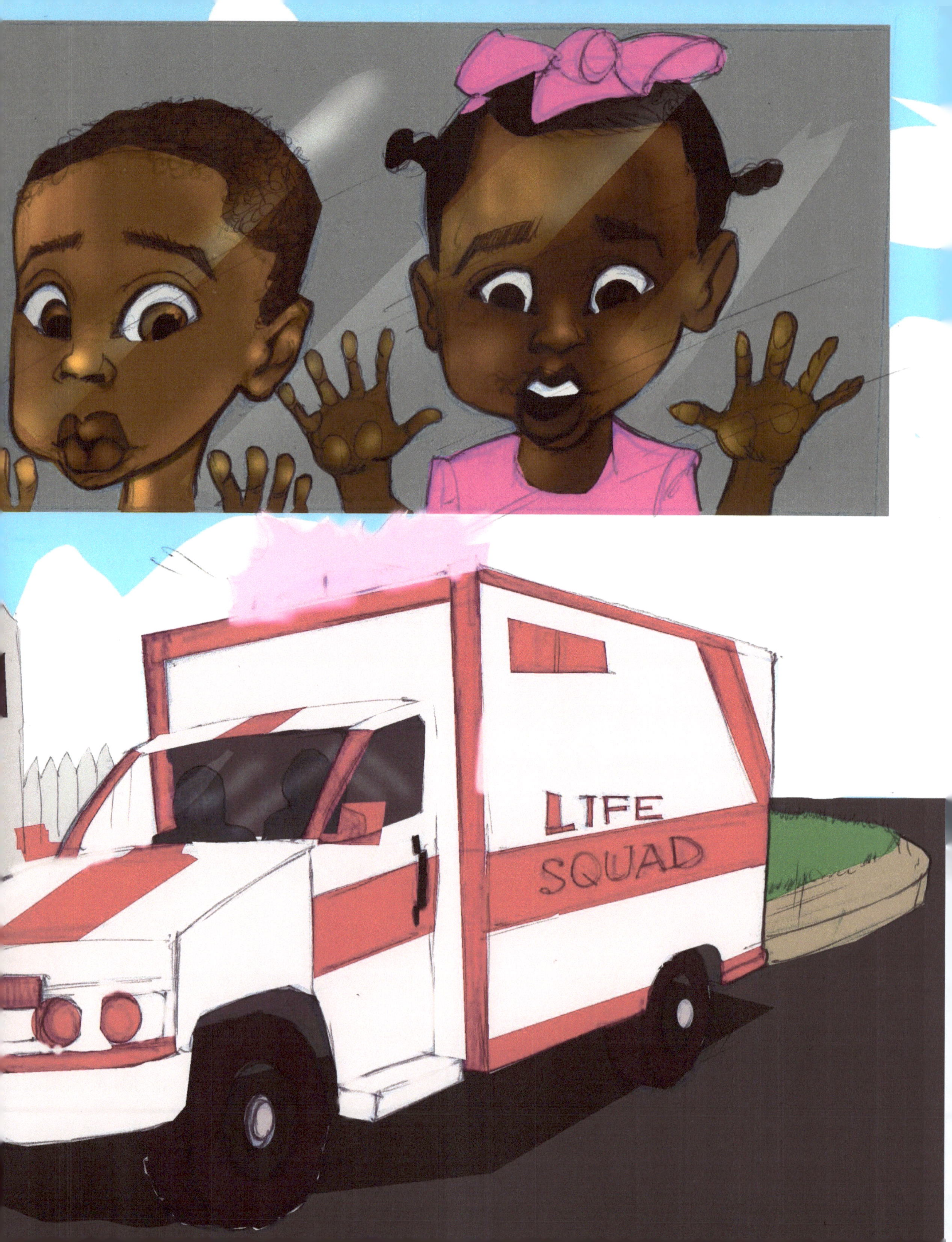
LIFE
SQUAD

Scene 14:

(MARIAH): "The lights are flashing, the horn is blowing! They're coming, it's the life squad Auntie Kisha! They're here!"

(ERIC JR): "I wonder will mom scream or will she shout (ouch)! I want to go to the hospital with my mom!

Scene 15:

"Dr. Kim Haugabook! Calling Dr. Kim Haugabook, delivery room No. 7 is ready."

(DR. KIM HAUGABOOK): "Mrs. Jones, push! Here it comes and it's a beautiful baby girl!"

Scene 16:

(MOM): "Finally Vanessa is here!"

(ERIC): "Honey! She is beautiful!"

"YES! It's a girl! It's a girl!" The girls shouted.

Scene 17:

We're back, we're back

we're back because we're smart.

It's cool, it's cool

It's cool to stay in school

We're back at school. It's the right thing to do

One grade at a time, then that diploma will be mine.

Scene 18:

We will study hard and have fun and get good grades like A's and B's. Mom will be so proud and one day we can have our own business like grannie.

Scene 19:

After the diploma we will get a degree. I will help you and you can help me. We're going to different colleges, but we're still cousins and friends. We'll never grow apart, ever again.

Scene 20:

"Auntie Kizzy had a girl too!?"

(MARIAH): "Yeah."

(OLIVIA): "It's a girl's world."

www.ingramcontent.com/pod-product-compliance
Lightning Source LLC
LaVergne TN
LVHW072233080526
838199LV00115B/506